HIERONYMUS BOSCH

THE MOCKING OF CHRIST   Oil   26 5/8″ x 20 3/8″   *Courtesy the John G. Johnson Art Collection, Philadelphia*

Hieronimüs Bosch

by

HOWARD DANIEL

THE HYPERION PRESS

AND

DUELL, SLOAN, AND PEARCE

NEW YORK

THIS VOLUME
UNDER THE SUPERVISION OF
ANDRÉ GLOECKNER
WAS FIRST PUBLISHED MCMXLVII BY
THE HYPERION PRESS, NEW YORK.
THE TEXT WAS SET IN BASKERVILLE
BY McKELLAR AND PLATTS, NEW
YORK; COLOUR BLOCKS ENGRAVED
BY CLICHÉ UNION, PARIS; W. F.
SEDGWICK, LTD., LONDON; AND
STANDARD-KOPPEL ENGRAVING
COMPANY, NEW YORK. PRINTED BY
MARKETTE PRINTING COMPANY,
NEW YORK; BINDING BY TAUBER'S
BOOKBINDERY, NEW YORK; JACKET
DESIGNED BY CLAUDE DE REMUSAT,
PARIS.

ALLEGORICAL FANTASY Print, diameter 8 1/4"
The Metropolitan Museum of Art, New York

HIERONYMUS BOSCH

Fifteen generations of men have come and gone since the Netherlands painter, Hieronymus Bosch, first opened a window into Hell and made the voyage around man's unconscious mind in a glass-bottomed boat. After more than four centuries of neglect Bosch now has special significance partly because all unknowingly he sired those refugees from reason, the surrealists, and partly for his extraordinary graphic qualities. One glimpse of a Bosch hell says as much as thirty-two cantos of Dante or twelve books of Milton.

The surrealists bear out once more the wisdom of Ecclesiastes that there is no new thing under the sun. What they have to say is the pale echo of what was said by Hieronymus Bosch four hundred and fifty years earlier. Of course the resemblance begins and ends on the surface. While the surrealists lifted many of their startling ideas and tricks from Bosch, their Freudian-loaded works would have been as thoroughly disturbing to Bosch as to most of us, their contemporaries.

And yet these almost incidental surrealist characteristics of Bosch—the smoke and fire of devastating Hell, violent death, the nightmare to end all nightmares, the landscapes and weird constructions disappearing into infinity—make him so interesting to the people of our troubled world. In the past Bosch has been obscured in the shadows cast by that team of artistic giants which began with the Van Eycks and ended with Brueghel.

Perhaps the contemporary interest in the bizarre and sensational will help to establish Bosch where the art historians have failed.

The schizoid nature of our modern civilization accents motion (no matter the direction), violence, and sensation. The opportunism of its commercialized culture points up the instability of its ideas and its idealogues; these are subject to rapid change as fashions in dress. These ingredients of our febrile age have certain outward and spiritual similarities with Bosch's times. Both ages are in-between periods of great instability and flux. The meaning and content of Bosch's art had special significance for his contemporaries but has practically none for us. He spoke to them in their own language. But to moderns the impact of the paintings comes from their form, color, and superficially surrealist aspects. They shock, surprise and stimulate us.

Time has worked great changes in Bosch's public. In his day he was a people's painter, his works immensely popular. Today he is essentially a painter's painter or an intellectual's painter.

The biographic details of this Professor Emeritus of the nightmare are as scanty as his panels are crowded. But there is no reason to assume that his own life in any way reflected the "anarchy-comes-to-the-nether-world" subject matter of his works. A careful study of Bosch's biographical potsherds and an even more careful study

[5]

of his paintings compels a belief that the normalcy and quietness of his life was in inverse proportion to the aberration and hell-clatter of his painted underworld.

To those who lay great store by biographical minutiæ Bosch will be a disappointment. Practically nothing of his life has come down to us beyond these incredible paintings. His full name, Hieronymus Bosch Van Aeken, suggests that his people came from Aachen but that he was a native of 's Hertogenbosch, a quiet little Brabant city in southern Holland.

Van Mander's *Schilderboeck*—a valuable account of the lives of Dutch and Flemish painters—is brief and vague. Writing about eighty years after the death of Bosch he had to pad his biography with some notes on the painter's technique:

"Jeronimus Bon Van Aken was born at 's Hertogenbosch. He painted gruesome pictures of spooks and horrid phantoms of hell... His treatment of draperies differs from that of earlier artists, who painted many wrinkles and folds. His technique was sure and clever and he painted *à la prima*. That is why his paintings remain unchanged and why they are in beautiful condition. As other old masters had done, he made his drawings of subjects on the white ground of his panel, over which he painted a transparent layer in a color, or in a shade, more or less like flesh. Frequently he used the ground for part of the final effect of the painting."

This brief note is concluded with a description and comment on a number of Bosch works which have been lost.

A more interesting report on Bosch appears in the Flemish painter-poet Lampsonius, a sort of sixteenth century Edgar Guest. Writing about fifty years

THE CROWNING WITH THORNS
Oil 29 1/4″ x 23 1/4″   *National Gallery, London*

after Bosch's death, he plays up the hell theme:

"Jeroon Bos, what is the meaning of your frightened face, of your pale features?

It looks as if you imagined all the spirits from hell were flying round your ears.

I could think you had listened to the roaring depths of Pluto's domain;

I could imagine the gates of hell had been opened to you.

You were so eminent an artist that you were able to paint all that has been enclosed in deepest hell."

Literary digging in the musty records of 's Hertogenbosch by such historians as Ebeling and Mosman has brought to light little pay dirt. A great deal of labor reveals only that Bosch was born about 1450 and died in 1516; that he sketched designs for the stained glass windows in the great town cathedral of St. John and helped with several altar paintings; that he belonged to the puritanical and semi-religious Brotherhood of Our Lady; that he was married and owned a house on the market place.

The only other tangibles we have amongst the biographical assets are some self-portraits, the most important being the drawing of Bosch as an old man from the Arras Code. Bosch, as a younger man, painted himself into several of his large works. Thus, in the Lisbon *Temptation of St. Anthony* he is the pale-faced monk crossing the bridge. In the right wing of the Escurial triptych, *The Garden of Earthly Delights*, it is surely Bosch's face looking out from under the table, a lost soul in hell. In an engraving after Bosch, *The Floating Tree*, his portrait is worked into the left side of the tree. No doubt the astrologists, tea-cup readers and the physiog-

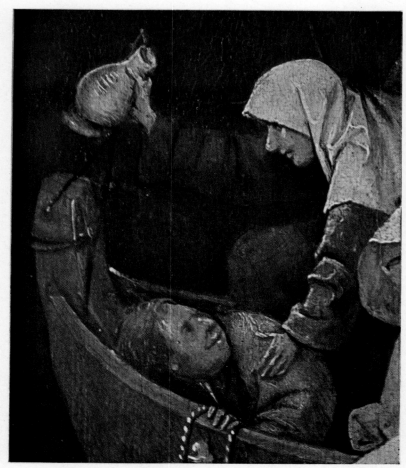

THE SHIP OF FOOLS   detail page 15
Louvre Museum, Paris

nomists could tell us all about Bosch from these portraits. For our purposes, however, it is enough to mark the great sensitivity of the melancholic, haunted face. Remark too, the bold, sure, modern technique of the painting and drawing.

The name of Bosch's teacher is unknown. The conjecture that he learned technique from one of the top-flight workshops in Delft or Haarlem is reasonable. Reasonable too, is the artistic linking of Bosch to the Delft Master of the *Virgo inter Virgines* and even to Robert Campin. However, while it is clear that Bosch is made-in-the-Netherlands, it is equally clear that he got little from his teachers but straight technique. From that point, Bosch is on his own, a lonely Cortes on some surrealist peak surveying the Oceans of Beyond Reality and with his sharp-focus telescope musing over what was happening to whom in the worst of all possible Hells. The ingredients for his devil's brew he found at hand, particularly in the Satans and Chimeras carved in stone and wood in his own Cathedral of St. John at 's Hertogenbosch. The recipe was entirely his own.

Unrest, conflict, and change are the characteristics which fairly flow out of Bosch's works. Consciousness of great social change and its powerful reflection in his

THE SHIP OF FOOLS   detail page 15
Louvre Museum, Paris

[8]

work separates Bosch from his contemporaries and even elevates him above them. In this, he is a lodestone pointing the way for the mighty Brueghel and for almost all later genre painters and explorers of the grotesque, Cranach, Callot, Hogarth, Goya, Doré, Rops, Kley, Kubin, Ensor, Art Young, and others.

The solid body of his artistic output is permeated by this sense of change. The significance of the impact of the major social forces of his day and what he learned from the changing world he lived in is meaningful to our more socially-conscious world. Indeed, the study of Bosch is only fruitful if set in a social and historical frame. In order to lay the ground, then, let us briefly survey this period which might well be called the Indian Summer of the Middle Ages.

To get Bosch into historical perspective, and indeed, to understand his completely bizarre quality we must know the world which produced him. By the middle of the fifteenth century, feudalism in north-western Europe was beginning to come apart at the seams. A way of life which had acted as a cohesive for so many centuries was now plainly dying. As this great system came to its close it produced in him the death-rattle of the Middle Ages. Cultural stock-takers like Bosch sum up much of what has gone before and create new forms and substances for those who come after.

In north-west Europe the Black Death, war, famine, pestilence, and other camp followers of the Four Horsemen had spurred man into heavy intellectual exercise outside the oppressive confines of the official Church.

THE SEVEN DEADLY SINS   Oil 21 3/4″ x 34″
Courtesy Tomas Harris, London

Individualism was developing. This period overlapping Bosch was the time of Wycliffe, Huss, and Luther. Society was in a state of the greatest flux. Ideas and men were in ferment. Here was a historical period when those who produced man's earthly goods staked out a claim to some of the products of their sweat and toil. This was the period of the Peasants Rising in England, the Jacquerie in France, Žižka and the Hussite wars in Bohemia and later the Peasant's war in Germany, and the Peasant Rising of Dozsa in Hungary.

Awareness of the break-up of feudalism with its set patterns of life brought on a tremendous sense of un-certainty and pessimism. Chancellor Gerson of the University of Paris, was sufficiently struck by the fervors, hysterics, and superstitions of his time to record his general impression that the world must be approaching its end. Read, too, how the chronicler of the glittering Burgundian Court, Chastellain, starts his narrative "I, man of sadness, born in an eclipse of darkness and thick fogs of lamentation. . ."

Bosch lived through the period when the glory of the Burgundians was sinking like a golden sunset, when that crafty old double-crosser, Louis XI, was hammering France into the rough image of a modern national state,

THE SHIP OF FOOLS　　　detail page 15
Louvre Museum, Paris

ticularly by contemporary chronicles. From most of Bosch's artistic contemporaries and predecessors there is a clear picture of one part of the life and times they worked in, but from the outside. Bosch tells this story, too. However in addition he sheds light on the inner life of his time. The sharp-minded Spanish monk, Joseph de Siguença, noted this fact about Bosch when cataloguing the paintings of the psychopathic Philip II:

> The difference which, according to me, exists between the paintings of this man and those of others, lies in the fact that the others aspired to paint man as he is externally; only he (Bosch) had the audacity to paint the inner man.

This is the period of the breakdown of city states and the interregnum preceding the establishment of the modern national state. Economic developments, such as "money" and new methods for the productive use of capital, thrust up a body of rich merchants and a large working class. Simultaneously they pushed down feudal nobles, anachronistic in their tarnished, moth-eaten chivalry, undermined the town guilds and shook to its foundations the great, rich, sprawling Church. All these pressures and conflicting interests created a combustible mixture which could and did ignite into violent explosion at a hot word. Bosch appeared when the patterns of modern times were forming. Much of his significance stems directly from his recognition not only of change but of the necessity for it.

Some institutions and concepts of the late Middle Ages which shaped peoples' mental and physical lives seem quite strange today. Amongst those which show up prominently in Bosch's works we note first the fixation on the idea of Hell. Four of his major paintings, the Lisbon *Temptation of St. Anthony*, the Escurial *Hay Wagon* and *Garden of Earthly Delights*, and the Vienna *Last Judgment* are wholly or partly sulphurous. While this fixation rides high in the mediæval mind, it got an extra leavening in Bosch's imagination through his contact with Alain de la Roche, inspirer of the celebrated Malleus Maleficarium—the fifteenth-century Who's Who amongst Witches. The infernal visions of this mystic were well known throughout the semi-religious order to which Bosch belonged.

The daily lunches of the Brotherhood at 's Hertogenbosch could hardly have been followed by postprandial bliss when we learn that they were enlivened by selected readings from *De quatuor hominum novissimis*, Denis the Carthusian's tabulation of Hell's horrors.

As if the terrors of everyday life were not enough—plague, typhus, and that endemic scourge of the Middle Ages, leprosy—the citizens had to scare themselves witless with superstitions not the least of which were witches. At one time or another there were witch trials going on which would have warmed Cotton Mather's icy heart. The midnight whirring of broomsticks

when the flourishing, independent cities of the Low Countries, the commercial center of the world, had just extracted the Groot Privilegie or Dutch Magna Charta from the unwilling Burgundians, and when the Hapsburgs were just beginning their endless intrigues and marriages in this part of the world.

The process of social, political, and intellectual life in the fifteenth - and sixteenth-century Lowlands was conditioned and even determined by contemporary modes of production which, at that time, were feudal. The economic and social forms frozen for so many centuries by this feudal system were now beginning to crack up in a great thaw. In the teeming Low Countries, the landed wealth of the Church and the great and prosperous textile industry of the Flemish-Brabant cities were the basic economic facts of life. The dominant class of burghers, international traders, Burgundian rulers and high clerics, all had their economic base in the textile trade.

Thus, from the van Eycks until Bosch, painting reflects the burgher ideal of prosperity, self-satisfaction, and orderliness. Bosch is an extraordinarily interesting exception to the general rule that the paintings of this last flowering of the middle ages were serene and happy. To get the true taste and smell of mediæval life the graphic arts have to be corrected by literature, par-

throbbed in Bosch's ears. The Lisbon *Temptation of St. Anthony* is a good example of how Bosch liked to fill in sky space with witchlike creatures floating across scenes of devastation. Bosch sucked in this brimstone-tainted air with his mother's milk and indelible impressions must have been left on his mind by such events as the seven-week sack of neighboring Liège in 1468 when Charles the Bold went through it like a bulldozer, leaving nothing standing but pillaged churches.

This was an age when rulers were blatant and unashamed in handing out plums to their bastard children. To Bosch it must have been double poison that the Bishop of near-by Utrecht was generally the bastard of whoever wore the Burgundian purple.

Just as the modern city dweller slakes his blood lust at a boxing match, his fifteenth-century counterpart in the Netherlands might hie him to the market square to see a "heretic" being given extreme therapy. Motley describes one such typical spectacle, an unfortunate who was flayed from neck to navel "while swarms of bees were let loose to fasten upon his bleeding flesh and torture him to a death of exquisite agony."

This was an age of incredible cruelty. Justice, that great and noble word, wore strange garb in the fifteenth and sixteenth centuries. Truth was coaxed out of people by the rack. As for punishment, once guilt had been "established," an ordinary hanging would almost be pleasurable to a victim who might have the choice made for him of expiring over a slow fire, being broken on a wheel, boiled in water or oil, pierced on a stake, burned alive, or merely torn apart by horses. Light punishment might take in branding, scourging, or the lopping off of fingers, hands, or ears. Understandably then, cruelty, often soaked in sadism, is a frequent theme with Bosch. The Hell paintings featuring knives, torture, fire, monsters, and devastation, have already been mentioned. The further development of this theme, with greater emphasis on the psychological aspects, is seen in the various versions of *The Crowning with Thorns*, *The Carrying of the Cross*, *Christ before Pilate*, and *Ecce Homo*.

Most of the thematic material appearing in Bosch's paintings is an inheritance of things past. But after it has been distilled in the metal test-tubes of his quite extraordinary personality, and bathed in that intensity of purpose which characterizes all great artists, it is new and fresh.

The shock of recognition that society was really dynamic produced a discernable trauma in the more sensitive minds of the day. Bosch is unclear as to the meaning of many of these changes and so we find him a self-appointed Jeremiah spelling out his theme—"the harvest is past, the summer is ended and we are not saved yet."

His greatest follower, Brueghel, appeared after enough time had elapsed to set the new age in some sort

SELF-PORTRAIT   Print
Arras Index

of perspective. That outward static appearance of mediæval life had quite melted away in him. By contrast, therefore, his is a more human art, forward-looking and optimistic even if sometimes ironical.

The psychology of this period has been nowhere better summarized than by the Dutch historian Huizinga when he writes: "So violent and ugly was life that it bore the mixed smell of blood and roses. The men of that time always oscillated between the fear of Hell and the most naive joy, between cruelty and tenderness, between harsh asceticism and insane attachments to the delights of this world, between hatred and goodness, always running to extremes."

Bosch forms part of a movement which has been in progress for centuries in Western Europe, a movement of spiritual reform (itself a reflection of changing economical life) which in the North crystallized in Erasmus, and after Bosch's death, in Luther and the Reformation. The wealth and power accumulated by the Church was accompanied by vicious abuses. Those devout Christians whose organized opposition offered a threat to the lords of creation oftimes drowned in their own blood. So perished the Albigensian and Waldensian "heretics."

MVLTÆ TRIBVLATIONES IVSTORVM DE OMNIBVS IIS LIBERABIT EOS DOMINVS · PSAL · 33 ·

TEMPTATION OF ST. ANTHONY   Print 13 x 16 7/8"
The Metropolitan Museum of Art, New York

The thin stream of ecclesiastical and moral reform began to gain momentum and body as it surged down to such mystics as Thomas à Kempis, and on to social critics like Brant and Erasmus. An important organization pushed up by this movement in the Netherlands was the Brotherhood of Common Life. Closely related to it was the 's Hertogenbosch Brotherhood of Our Lady, attached to the Cathedral of St. John. This was a puritanical, reform society devoted to good works.

Erasmus, who lived for a time at 's Hertogenbosch, was, like Bosch, connected with this organization. Whether or not the two were in contact, they shared a common interest in the fascinating subject of Folly. This was an important part of the intellectual stock of ideas in the late Middle Ages and early northern renaissance. Many intellectuals were absorbed in its contemplation. Sebastian Brant would have us believe that the malady was universal, when in his *Ship of Fools* he writes:

Think not we fools are all alone,
For brothers large and small we own,
In every country everywhere,
Our ranks are swelled beyond compare.

Erasmus was particularly exercised about the fools in Bosch's home district. In his *In Praise of Folly* he remarks: "And rightly do we bruit it about concerning the people of Brabant, that although time brings prudence to others, the older Brabanters grow the more foolish they are." Bosch's intimate knowledge and interest in this subject is revealed by his painting *The Ship of Fools*.

Another literary work which had wide influence for several centuries and provided thematic material for Bosch was the *Vision of Tondale*. This precursor of Dante unfolds the dream of an Irish knight who was taken on a Cook's Tour of Hell and other regions of the soul. The ingenuous message of this jaunt through the Mediæval Chamber of Horrors is that sin does not pay. Much of the

[12]

Hieronymus·Bos·Inuentor· · Æ · *Cock excudebat·1559·*
cum gratia et priuilegio

Daer pl<platbroeck> speelman is en stierman in de bane | En al tiert syn ghesselscay datse moghen sweeten
Daer sien hem de voghelen voer eenen huyben ane | Het sullen de sanghers in de blau schuyte heeten

THE BLUE SHIP   Print 9 x 11 3/4"
The Metropolitan Museum of Art, New York

atmosphere of Bosch's *Hells* and *Last Judgments* comes from works such as this. The scene of a man riding a cow across the bridge in the right wing of the Escurial *Hay Wagon* is Tondale's account of the punishment meted out to the sacrilegious.

His penchant for didactic literature is clear, and doubtless the mediæval mystery play influenced him. In the 's Hertogenbosch Brotherhood he probably attended to the artistic management of many plays. His several versions of *Christ Bearing the Cross* are possibly based on local passion plays. In turn, didacticism is a strong motif in all his paintings. He tried to make his paintings comprehensible to souls as simple as François Villon's mother:

In my parish church I see Paradise painted,
Where are harps and lutes: and a hell
Where the damned are boiled.
The one frightens me, the other brings
Joy and gladness.

Another great mediæval source book and inspiration for artists was the *Golden Legend*. Many of Bosch's paintings are illustrations from this universally popular collection of lives of the Saints. The various versions of the *Temptation of St. Anthony*, the *Martyrdom of St. Julia*, the *St. John at Patmos*, and the *St. Jerome* are inspired by this book. Of course Bosch always injects himself into these works, and where the flora and fauna are not from the *Bestiaries* they are from his own rich imagination. The fantastic animals which parade through the *Garden of Earthly Delights* come directly or indirectly from the *Bestiaries* and from St. John's *Apocalypse*, that white-hot warning to wantons.

In an age where art and the people were on intimate terms the world was untroubled by non-objective art. Painting was essentially literary, usually sacred but sometimes profane. One of the great profane influences was the monumental *Romance of the Rose*, a thirteenth-

[13]

century encyclopaedia of love, legend and ritual. This rich allegory full of bizarre landscape and weird symbolic figures was regarded as heretical and the controversy over it gave off more heat than a uranium oven. It is the key to the mysteries of such paintings as the *Garden of Earthly Delights*. In this work Bosch, like a northern Savanarola, appointed himself a one-man purge commission to safeguard Christian orthodoxy. His objective was the moral delousing of a sinful citizenry.

The triptych must be studied as a whole, the open wings and the reverse of the folded wings. The folded wings show the undefiled globe, the left wing the Creation and Fall, and the big center panel the great Rose Garden of sin in which mankind is wallowing. Finally, the stupendous right wing depicts the inevitable Hell at the end of Pleasure Road.

He uses this simple pattern a number of times. Another magnificent triptych, the Escurial *Hay Wagon* has the same arrangement. The left wing is a serene Garden of Eden with the Temptation and Fall. The center panel is a gigantic hay wagon. This symbol of the sinful world is an illustration of the Netherlands proverb "the world is a pile of hay; each takes what he can grab." The right wing Hell is Bosch at his diabolical best.

A more personal example of Bosch's concern for social comment is his great painting, *The Prodigal Son*. While there is no agreement that the subject is the prodigal son, there can be no dispute about the painting being a masterwork of the first quality. The sign of the swan hanging from the broken-down inn is a clue to the meaning of this picture. The swan was the symbol of the Brotherhood of Our Lady, Bosch's religious fraternity. He is expressing his extreme pessimism about the state of the world. The Brotherhood, represented by the decayed building, has turned out to be a disappointment. The sad and disillusioned center figure—possibly a self-portrait—will seek salvation elsewhere. Something new has been added to northern painting. Here are shadows of the coming Brueghel.

An evaluation of Bosch is a complicated task. He had no school and only a few obscure followers like Mandyn and Huys. And yet his influence was tremendous. His strong and obvious influence on Brueghel is enough of itself to give him immortality. The list of his major contributions to the history of art is imposing. He is one of the first of the landscape painters. Some of the non-fantastic landscapes which he uses as back-drops have more than enough merit to stand on their own. Note, in this regard, the Prado and Johnson collection *Adoration of the Magi* and the Berlin *St. John at Patmos*. His many studies of human bodies in motion, something quite novel, opened up new fields and made possible much of Brueghel's work. He is a master draftsman whose drawing can stand comparison with the work of any of his contemporaries. He is the introducer of genre into northern painting as well as being the introducer of diablerie, the bizarre, and grotesque. He is thus in many ways the artistic father of a host of subsequent masters. As a colorist he is supreme, perhaps the best of the whole northern renaissance. His startling colors, sometimes exquisitely beautiful, always clear and jewel-like, contribute greatly to the psychological atmosphere of his works. His mastery of the sombre, dark colors associated with the fires of devastation has never been surpassed.

Finally, we must take note of perhaps his greatest contribution. Realism in painting—and it had reached its apogee in the north—was deepened and enriched by the penetrating psychological approaches which he introduced. There has never been a painter before or since who has so thoroughly and deeply explored the fear and guilt caverns of man's inner life. And in this regard there is a modernity about him which has been underlined by the developments in the field of psychoanalysis and abnormal psychology and in the whole surrealist movement. From this remarkable master of the nightmare we have for the first time in art mature, incisive, social criticism.

HOWARD DANIEL

THE SHIP OF FOOLS   Oil   22 1/6″ x 12 4/5″
Louvre Museum, Paris

THE MOCKING OF CHRIST   Oil   20 1/2" x 21 1/4"
Courtesy the John G. Johnson Art Collection, Philadelphia

ADORATION OF THE MAGI   Oil   30 1/2" x 22"
Courtesy of the John G. Johnson Art Collection, Philadelphia

GARDEN OF EARTHLY DELIGHTS: *Garden of Eden*
Oil   Left wing   *Escorial, Madrid*

THE HAY WAGON: Triptych   Center panel   Oil   53" x 39 1/4"
Escorial, Madrid

GARDEN OF EARTHLY DELIGHTS   Center panel of Triptych
Oil 86 3/8″ x 76 1/2″
Escorial, Madrid

THE HAY WAGON: Creation, Temptation, and Flight
Detail page 19   Left wing   Oil   53″ x 17 7/8″
Escorial, Madrid

THE HAY WAGON: Hell
Detail page 19   Right wing   Oil   53″ x 17 7/8″
Escorial, Madrid

THE HAY WAGON   Detail page 19, center panel
Escorial, Madrid

THE HAY WAGON   Detail page 19, center panel
Escorial, Madrid

GARDEN OF EARTHLY DELGHTS: *Hell*
Escorial, Madrid

Detail page 26

THE BETRAYAL OF CHRIST   Glazed tempera   20″ x 32″
The Fine Arts Gallery of San Diego

GARDEN OF EARTHLY DELIGHTS
Escorial, Madrid

Detail page 20, center panel

GARDEN OF EARTHLY DELIGHTS: Hell
Detail right wing
Escorial, Madrid

GARDEN OF EARTHLY DELIGHTS: Hell
Right wing
Escorial, Madrid

CHRIST DERIDED   Oil   76 1/4" x 64 5/8"
Escorial, Madrid

THE CROWNING WITH THORNS detail page 7 *National Gallery, London*

TEMPTATION OF ST. ANTHONY   Oil 16 1/2″ x 10 1/4″

E. and A. Silberman Galleries, New York

CHRIST BEFORE PILATE   Oil   31 1/4″ x 41″
Museum of Historic Art, Princeton University

ARRIVAL OF THE MAGI   Right wing of an Adoration of the Magi

Oil   14 1/4″ x 8 3/8″

Courtesy the John G. Johnson Art Collection, Philadelphia

THE LAST JUDGMENT   Center panel   Oil   64″ x 50 1/8″
Academy of Fine Arts, Vienna

Oil   23 1/2″ x 44 3/4″   *Old Pinakothek, Munich*

ADORATION OF THE SHEPHERDS　　Left wing of an Adoration of the Magi
Oil　14 3/8″ x 8 7/8″
Courtesy the John G. Johnson Art Collection, Philadelphia

THE LAST JUDGMENT   Detail page 32, center panel
Academy of Fine Arts, Vienna

THE EPIPHANY Oil Triptych Center panel 54 1/4″ x 28 3/8″
Wings 54 1/4″ x 13″
Prado, Madrid

THE SEVEN DEADLY SINS Detail page 9
Courtesy Tomas Harris, London

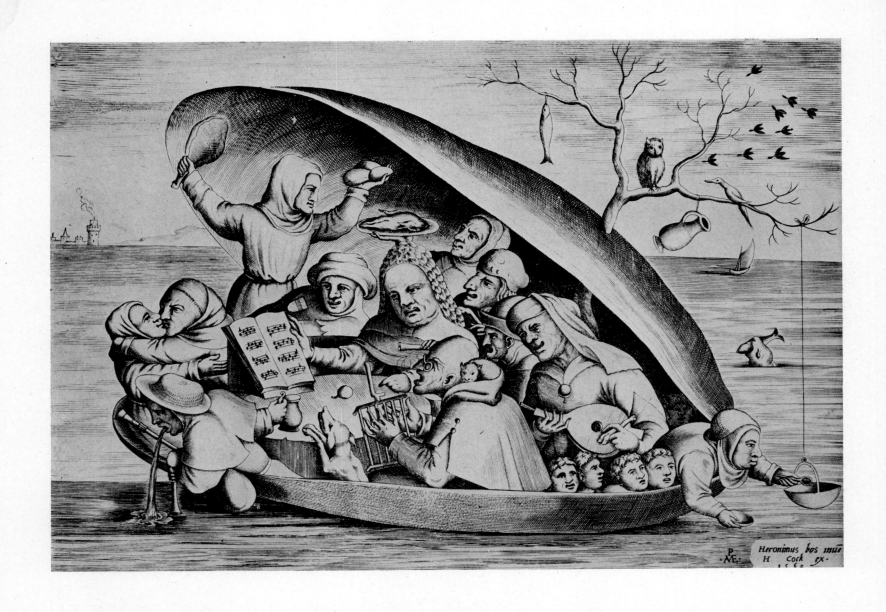

SATIRICAL PRINT   8 1/2″ x 11 3/8″

The Metropolitan Museum of Art, New York

[40]

ECCE HOMO   Oil   29 1/2″ x 24″
Art Institute, Frankfort-on-the-Main

TEMPTATION OF ST. ANTHONY Center panel of triptych
Oil 51 1/2″ x 46 3/8″
National Museum, Lisbon

TEMPTATION OF ST. ANTHONY   Detail
Oil
Rijksmuseum, Amsterdam

TEMPTATION OF ST. ANTHONY
Detail page 42, center panel
National Museum, Lisbon

TEMPTATION OF ST. ANTHONY
Detail of left wing
National Museum, Lisbon

TEMPTATION OF ST. ANTHONY
Left wing of triptych   Oil   51 1/2″ x 20″
National Museum, Lisbon

TEMPTATION OF ST. ANTHONY
Detail page 44
National Museum, Lisbon

TEMPTATION OF ST. ANTHONY
Detail page 44
National Museum, Lisbon

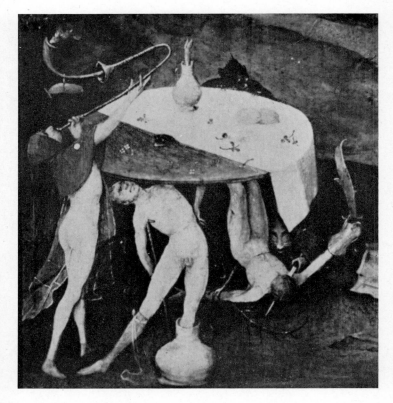

TEMPTATION OF ST. ANTHONY
Detail of right wing
National Museum, Lisbon

TEMPTATION OF ST. ANTHONY
Right wing of triptych   Oil   51 1/2″ x 20″
National Museum, Lisbon

TEMPTATION OF ST. ANTHONY   Detail page 46
National Museum, Lisbon

TEMPTATION OF ST. ANTHONY
National Museum, Lisbon

Detail page 46

TEMPTATION OF ST. ANTHONY
National Museum, Lisbon

Detail page 46

TEMPTATION OF ST. ANTHONY
Right wing, reverse   Oil   51 1/2″ x 20″
National Museum, Lisbon

TEMPTATION OF ST. ANTHONY
Left wing, reverse   Oil   51 1/2″ x 20″
National Museum, Lisbon

TEMPTATION OF ST. ANTHONY
Detail page 50
National Museum, Lisbon

TEMPTATION OF ST. ANTHONY
Detail page 50
National Museum, Lisbon

TEMPTATION OF ST. ANTHONY　　　　　　Oil　27 1/2″ x 20″
Prado, Madrid

THE CONJURER Oil 23 1/2" x 28 1/4"
Municipal Museum, St. Germain-en-Laye

CHRIST CARRYING THE CROSS   Oil 22 3/8″ x 12 5/8″
Kunsthistorisches Museum, Vienna

SELECTED BIBLIOGRAPHY

BOOKS

BRANT, S. The Ship of Fools ("Das Narrenschiff"). Tr. from the German by E. Zeydel. New York, Columbia Univ. Press, 1944.

CONWAY, M. The Van Eycks and Their Followers. London, Murray, 1921.

DUPONT, J. Jérôme Bosch. Le retable de Saint Antoine du Musée National de Lisbonne. Brussels, Editions de la Connaissance, 1937.

ELST, J. van der. The Last Flowering of the Middle Ages. New York, 1944.

EPHRON, W. Hieronymus Bosch — zwei Kreuztragungen. Vienna & Leipzig, Amathea-Verlag, c1931, plates.

ERASMUS, D. Praise of Folly. Tr. by H. Hudson. Princeton, Princeton Univ. Press, 1941.

FIERENS-GEVAERT, H. Les Primitifs Flamands, in La Peinture en Belgique. Vol. 3, pp. 169-181, six plates. Brussels, G. van Oest & Co., 1910.

FOURCAUD, L. de. Hieronymus van Aken dit Jérôme Bosch. Paris, G. Baranger Fils, 1912.

FRIEDLANDER, M. Hieronymus Bosch: Leben und Werke, in Die altniederländische Malerei. Vol. 5, pp. 79-130. Berlin, P. Cassirer, 1927.

FRIEDLANDER, M. Von Eyck bis Bruegel. Berlin, J. Bart, 1921.

GOSART, M. La Peinture de diableries à la fin du Moyen Age: Jérôme Bosch le "faizeur de Dyables" de bois-le Duc. Lille, Imprimerie Centrale du Nord, 1907.

GUEVARA, D. FELIPE DE. Comentarios de la pintura. Madrid, 1788.

HUEBNER, F. M. Hieronymus Bosch. Berlin, A. Juncker, 1938.

HUIZINGA, J. The Waning of the Middle Ages. London, E. Arnold, 1927.

LAFOND, P. Hieronymus Bosch: son art, son influence, ses disciples. Brussels, G. van Oest & Co., 1914.

MAETERLINCK, L. Le Genre satirique dans la peinture flamande. Brussels, G. Van Oest, 1907.

MANDER, C. van. Dutch and Flemish Painters. New York, McFarlaine, 1931.

MOSMANS, J. De St. Janskerk te 's Hertogenbosch. 's Hertogenbosch, 1931.

PFISTER, K. Hieronymus Bosch. Potsdam, G. Kiepenheumer, 1922.

SCHUBERT-SOLDERN, F. von. Hieronymus Bosch and P. Breugel. Vienna, 1903.

SCHURMEYER, W. Hieronymus Bosch. Munich, R. Piper & Co., 1923.

TOLNAY, C. de. Hieronymus Bosch. Bâle, Ed. Holbein, 1937.

VALENTINER, W. Catalogue of J. G. Johnson Collection. See "Flemish and Dutch Paintings," Vol. II, Nos. 352-353, illustrated. Philadelphia, J. G. Johnson, 1913.

WAGNER, H. Tondale's Visions. Halle, 1893.

PERIODICALS

BALDASS, L. von. "Betrachtungen zum Werke des Hieronymus Bosch," in Jahrbuch der kunsthistorischen Sammlungen in Wien. A. Schroll Verlag, 1926, N. S., Vol. I: pp. 103-122, illustrated, plates.

BALDASS, L. von. "Die Chronologie der Gemälde des Hieronymus Bosch," in Jahrbuch der preussischen Kunstsammlungen. Berlin, 1917, Vol. 38: pp. 177-195, illustrated.

BREDT, E. von KUBIN. "Bosch und Klinger," in die Kunst für Alle. München, F. Bruckmann, Vol. 38, pp. 293-304.

BRION, M. "Le Sentiment de la vie de Jérôme Bosch," in Beaux-Arts, Paris, Sept. 16, 1938, pp. 1-3.

BRION, M. "Le Singe de Dieu: Hieronymus Bosch," in Renaissance, Jan. 1939, Vol. 21, pp. 17-31, 49.

COHEN, W. "Hieronymus Bosch," article in Thieme and Becker. Allgemeines Lexikon der bildenden Künstler von der Antike bis zur Gegenwart. Leipzig, W. Engelmann Verlag, Vol. 4, 1910, pp. 386-389. With bibliography and list of works.

DOLLMAYR, H. "Hieronymus Bosch, und die Darstellung der vier letzten Dinge in der Niederländischen Malerei des XV. und XVI. Jahrhunderts," in Jahrbuch der Kunsthistorischen Sammlungen. Wien, 1898, Vol. 19, pp. 284-343, illustrated, plates.

GAUNT, W. "Fifteenth Century Surrealist: Hieronymus Bosch," in London Studio, Oct. 1938, Vol. 16, pp. 189-196, illustrated, color plates.

GLUCK, G. "Zu einem Bilde von H. Bosch in der Figdorschen Sammlung," in Jahrbuch der preussischen Kunstsammlungen. Berlin, 1905.

JUSTI, C. "Die Werke des H. Bosch in Spanien," in Jahrbuch der preussischen Kunstsammlungen. Berlin, Grote, 1889, Vol. 10, pp. 121-144.

ODENHEIMER, D. "The Garden of Paradise by Bosch," in Chicago Art Institute Bulletin. Dec. 1940, pp. 106-107, illustrated.

ODENHEIMER, D. "When Bosch dreamed of Paradise," (Unsigned review of Odenheimer's article, in Chicago Art Institute Bulletin, 1940) in Art Digest, N. Y., Hopell, Dec. 15, 1940, Vol. 15, p. 13.

PARROT, L. "La Flamme et la Cendre: Jérôme Bosch," in Formes et Couleurs. Lausanne, 1944.

SAIKO, G. "The Possibility of Symbolism in Modern Paintings," in Creative Art, Dec. 1931, Vol. 9, pp. 467-474.

SCHUBERT-SOLDERN, F. von. "Von Jan Van Eyk bis Hieronymus Bosch," in Studien zur deutschen Kunstgeschichte. Strassburg, Heitz, 1903, Vol. 46, pp. 99-109.

INDEX OF ILLUSTRATIONS

Color Plates are listed in italics